I0428821

CORRUPTION IN CHINA TODAY: CONSEQUENCES FOR GOVERNANCE, HUMAN RIGHTS, AND COMMERCIAL RULE OF LAW

ROUNDTABLE

BEFORE THE

CONGRESSIONAL-EXECUTIVE COMMISSION ON CHINA

ONE HUNDRED THIRTEENTH CONGRESS

FIRST SESSION

NOVEMBER 21, 2013

Printed for the use of the Congressional-Executive Commission on China

Available via the World Wide Web: http://www.cecc.gov

U.S. GOVERNMENT PRINTING OFFICE

86–657 PDF   WASHINGTON : 2014

For sale by the Superintendent of Documents, U.S. Government Printing Office
Internet: bookstore.gpo.gov   Phone: toll free (866) 512–1800; DC area (202) 512–1800
Fax: (202) 512–2104   Mail: Stop IDCC, Washington, DC 20402–0001

CONGRESSIONAL-EXECUTIVE COMMISSION ON CHINA

LEGISLATIVE BRANCH COMMISSIONERS

Senate

SHERROD BROWN, Ohio, *Chairman*
MAX BAUCUS, Montana
CARL LEVIN, Michigan
DIANNE FEINSTEIN, California
JEFF MERKLEY, Oregon

House

CHRISTOPHER SMITH, New Jersey,
   Cochairman
FRANK WOLF, Virginia
ROBERT PITTENGER, North Carolina
MARK MEADOWS, North Carolina
TIM WALZ, Minnesota
MARCY KAPTUR, Ohio
MICHAEL HONDA, California

EXECUTIVE BRANCH COMMISSIONERS

NISHA DESAI BISWAL, U.S. Agency for International Development

LAWRENCE T. LIU, *Staff Director*
PAUL B. PROTIC, *Deputy Staff Director*

(II)

CONTENTS

(III)

CORRUPTION IN CHINA TODAY: CONSEQUENCES FOR GOVERNANCE, HUMAN RIGHTS, AND COMMERCIAL RULE OF LAW

THURSDAY, NOVEMBER 21, 2013

CONGRESSIONAL-EXECUTIVE
COMMISSION ON CHINA,
Washington, DC.

The roundtable was convened at 3:05 p.m., in room SVC 209–208, Capitol Visitor Center, Lawrence Liu, Staff Director, presiding.

Present: Paul Protic, Deputy Staff Director and Anna Brettell, Senior Advisor.

OPENING STATEMENT OF LAWRENCE LIU, STAFF DIRECTOR, CONGRESSIONAL–EXECUTIVE COMMISSION ON CHINA

Mr. LIU. Thanks, everyone, for joining us today. I wanted to welcome you on behalf of our chair, Senator Sherrod Brown, to this CECC roundtable and introduce myself. My name is Lawrence Liu, and I am the Staff Director for the Commission.

To my left is Paul Protic, who works for Congressman Chris Smith, our cochair. Then to his left is Anna Brettell, our Senior Advisor, who has done great work in preparing for this roundtable.

I wanted to just introduce everyone to the topic real quickly and then introduce the witnesses, and then we can hear their remarks.

The topic of today's roundtable is corruption in China, which is a major source of discontent among the Chinese people and a barrier to commercial rule of law. Corruption takes many forms in China, from corrupt officials at all levels using their public office for private gain, and seizing land for development, to corrupt state-owned enterprises gaming the system to their advantage.

Corruption continues to be among the root causes of rights abuses against Chinese citizens. Chinese citizens have long voiced concern about corruption. In 1989, corruption was among the main reasons leading to massive citizen protests. Today, thousands of citizens file complaints and provide tips about corrupt practices.

Chinese leaders have also long voiced concern about the issue, linking the Party's legitimacy to its ability to manage corruption. For over 20 years, Party and government leaders have issued numerous laws, regulations, and policies to combat corruption.

Following some major corruption scandals last year, for example, President Xi Jinping himself launched a new anticorruption campaign, focusing especially on reducing very visible extravagant spending.

Despite these measures, corruption in China does remain rampant, raising important questions regarding the sincerity and effectiveness of these efforts, and ultimately whether China can be successful, given that it lacks free elections, a free press, an independent judiciary, and other checks and balances to hold officials accountable.

At the same time, officials continue to crack down on independent and citizen-led efforts to combat corruption, raising questions regarding the role the Chinese Government sees ordinary citizens playing in its campaign against corruption.

Finally, corruption in China raises important questions regarding China's commercial rule of law development, particularly with respect to China's powerful state-owned enterprises, who are a main source of corruption.

We have brought together a great group of panelists today who will address these questions. I will introduce them now and they will give their opening remarks, and then we'll have Q&A.

Our first speaker will be Joseph Fewsmith, a Professor of International Relations and Political Science at Boston University. Professor Fewsmith has written numerous articles published in well-known journals and is the author or editor of eight books, including most recently "The Logic and Limits of Political Reform in China." He is one of seven regular contributors to the China Leadership Monitor, a highly respected and widely read Web publication analyzing current developments in China. Thank you for joining us.

Our next speaker will be Xiaorong Li, an independent scholar who was a research faculty member at the University of Maryland, College Park. Her academic fields have included political philosophy and ethics, with a focus on human rights, democracy, and civil society development.

She has published numerous articles and books on these subjects. Since 1989, she has co-founded human rights organizations and has served as an executive director and a board member for those organizations, and she has also been a frequent contributor to our work. Thank you for joining us.

We will next hear from Andrew Wedeman, a Professor of Political Science at Georgia State University. Dr. Wedeman has published numerous articles and chapters and several books on corruption in China, including "Double Paradox: Rapid Growth and Rising Corruption in China." That book was selected by Foreign Affairs as one of the 30 best international relations books of 2012. Thank you for joining us.

Finally, we will hear from Daniel Chow, Joseph S. Platt-Porter, Wright, Morris & Arthur Professor of Law at Ohio State University's Michael E. Moritz College of Law. At Ohio State, Professor Chow writes and teaches in the areas of international trade, international business transactions, international intellectual property, and the law of China. He is the author of several leading casebooks in these areas, as well as many articles.

Previously, he lived in China and served as in-house counsel for a major U.S. corporation, where he handled all legal matters for the company and was involved firsthand in issues involving counterfeiting, commercial bribery, and government corruption. Thanks for joining us, Professor Chow.

So without further ado, Professor Fewsmith?

STATEMENT OF JOSEPH FEWSMITH, PROFESSOR OF INTER-NATIONAL RELATIONS AND POLITICAL SCIENCE, BOSTON UNIVERSITY

Mr. FEWSMITH. Thank you very much. It is a pleasure to be here this afternoon. Thank you for your invitation. I'll see what I can contribute to you in seven minutes.

The topic of corruption, I know, has gotten a lot of attention lately. There are a lot of sensational stories that are published and so forth, and I do think that some of those cases have had some serious impact on China as we see in the campaign that Lawrence Liu just mentioned of Xi Jinping launching his attack on corruption.

From what we can see in this early development of this campaign it may be the most serious and sustained attack against corruption in the last 30 years that I've been watching China. I'll get back to that in a minute.

But what I'd like to do is take the problem of corruption out of the headlines and look at it a little bit more in terms of the structure of the system because I think the problem of corruption is really deeply intertwined with the cadre evaluation system on the one hand, and the fiscal system on the other.

Local cadres are under a lot of pressure to develop their local economies. Higher levels are more concerned with what they do than how they do it. If some investment funds are diverted but tasks are still completed, then higher levels are generally willing to turn a blind eye.

It should be noted that this high-pressure system has had some real positive benefits for China. It is this system that has driven Chinese economic development over the last 30 years. The down side is it imbeds corruption into the fabric of the body politic.

The fiscal system is important because of the way it interacts with local government. For instance, the 1994 tax reform, which recentralized a lot of the taxes in China, left lower levels of government—and by "lower levels of government" I mean particularly the county, township, village levels—with fewer sources of funds, but the cadres remain under the same pressures to develop the local economies.

So now the job is what we in Washington might call an unfunded mandate, do the job, but you don't have the resources. Well, they need the resources, so where do they go and get the resources but from the peasants? So the central government mandate was that the agricultural tax, the tax on peasants, could not exceed 5 percent of income, but it regularly went up to 30, even 40 percent of income.

So you see the pressure the cadres are under to raise income so that they can do their jobs, and needless to say they also deploy some of those funds for themselves and for some of their colleagues.

I think that it is no coincidence that the number of so-called mass incidents took off roughly from this time forward. In 1993, there were, according to official figures, 8,700 mass incidents. In 2005, the last year that official figures were published, there were some 87,000 mass incidents, 10 times as many as a decade or so previously.

It is precisely this steady increase in local violence that led central authorities in 2006 to abolish the collection of the agricultural tax and miscellaneous fees. This was a major decrease in the financial burden on the peasants, but it also further reduced—even eliminated in some areas—the fiscal revenues of local government.

For those local townships that had no or little amount of industry as opposed to agricultural, elimination of the agricultural tax was disastrous. They were still under pressure, however, to develop their local economies but had no funds to do it with. But land was becoming a very precious commodity.

Industry was looking for places to expand, moving from the coast to the interior, or from coast to more of the interior even on coastal provinces. So land is becoming very valuable, so that's where you begin to get the reports of officials seizing property and giving peasants little or no compensation for that. Then they use the land to attract investment, and of course that becomes a major source of corruption.

So the number of mass incidents, surprisingly enough given that you have abolished the agricultural tax, has apparently continued to increase. There are no official statistics on this, but one widely cited figure put the number of mass incidents at 180,000 in 2010.

Besides the pressures from above to develop the economy, the temptation for corruption was simply enormous. Let me just cite one figure. In 2005, there were 163,000 hectares of state-owned land that were sold. One-third was sold through bidding, auction, in other words at market prices, while the other two-thirds were sold through non-market, non-transparent means.

The difference in price between the land sold openly at market prices and the land sold through non-market means was four to five times. That is a huge difference. It amounts to about 5 million renminbi per hectare, roughly $800,000 in U.S. dollar terms. That was just as land prices were taking off, so we have to assume that over the last nearly decade that that differential and the temptation to use the profits of that land have simply grown.

So the temptation to requisition land, sell it to investors, and pocket some of the proceeds was simply enormous and apparently it was not resisted by very many. The cadre system in China is a very hierarchical system and places a great deal of authority in the hands of Party secretaries at all levels.

In other words, there is a strong tendency toward a personalization of power at each level. Given the great power that comes with office, the temptation to simply buy and sell offices is great. For instance, one example is a Party secretary in a county in Shaanxi Province in the northwest that simply transferred 400 cadres at one time. When you see large personnel movements of that sort there is a great suspicion that that was in exchange for bribes, moving to more profitable ones.

A Party secretary in a county in Fujian transferred 545 cadres in several different batches. So in other words, you have all these Party secretaries that control personnel, and personnel want to move to more lucrative jobs so there is actual buying and selling of office.

Now, the recent third plenum that just ended about two weeks ago passed a decision that calls for increasing the power of the Discipline Inspection Commission, the watchdog, at each level of the Party.

The language of the decision is not entirely clear but it does say that the Discipline Inspection Commission at one level should have the primary responsibility for nominating the Discipline Inspection Commission head at the lower level. That would centralize or lift up, raise the level of responsibility.

It seems like, in Chinese terms, that they are changing the so-called professional relationship, this dual leadership system, and the leadership relationship, that those two are being reversed. It is not altogether clear at this point, but if so that is an important change in the organization of these things.

I mention this because that suggests that this campaign against corruption could really have some teeth to it. On the other hand, I will also say that this is not the first time that the Party has tried to strengthen the Discipline Inspection Commission and it has not worked in the past for a number of reasons, including the fact that if you have somebody who is basically over the local Party secretary then the Party system itself becomes disrupted, so they have always reverted to leaving the Party secretary in charge.

So I have to say that we have seen calls to crack down on corruption almost every year over the last 30 years. I just did not have time last night to go down to the basement and try to look up a speech that Hu Yaobang gave in 1986. I remember reading that at that time. It was a real barn-burner, you know: if we don't crack down on corruption the Party just cannot stand. Well, that was 30-plus years ago and we still have the same calls for crackdowns on corruption, and I think the urgency is at least as great.

So the record of the past three decades, of course, is really not very encouraging, so I think that the best we can really hope for in this present crackdown on corruption is slowing down the rate of growth in corruption.

Despite this change of the Discipline Inspection Commission, I just don't think that you can eliminate, or even significantly retard, corruption at the lower levels. As long as local cadres are being evaluated on their ability to develop the economy, there will be these pressures and they will continue to do as they have for the last three decades.

Thank you.

Mr. LIU. Thank you very much.

Ms. Li?

STATEMENT OF LI XIAORONG, INDEPENDENT SCHOLAR

Ms. LI. Thank you. That was a nice opening Professor Fewsmith, which sets up for what I'm about to say. I think the structural analysis that Professor Fewsmith emphasizes is very helpful. Somehow, maybe I will take it to a less optimistic conclusion than his.

Mr. FEWSMITH. That was optimistic?

Ms. LI. I'm going to discuss the connection between corruption and human rights abuses, and the ongoing crackdown on independent efforts to fight corruption, or more specifically, the puzzling behavior of the Chinese Government under the leadership of

Xi Jinping, who has himself vowed to clean up corruption, while his government is striking hard on anticorruption activists.

It is pretty obvious that government corruption is one of the important causes for some of the serious human rights violations in China today. If you have been watching what's going on, you may have wondered: Why are the officials and policemen so ferocious to the petitioners—petitioners are those who try to get a hearing from higher authorities about their grievances against local officials? Why? Because those who carry out the abduction, detention, those who run the "black jails," tend to be promised money. The money comes from local government officials who want to have petitioners from their own jurisdictions locked up in "black jails," threatened into submission until they stop petitioning. This is because local officials have so much at stake: their performances or political future depends on whether they could stop petitioners from telling on them to higher authorities. And the higher authorities also ordered them to stop the petitioners out of a fear of them as a source of threat and instability.

This is also why officials continue to force psychiatric institutions to take petitioners or activists, even after the new Mental Health Law was enacted, which bans involuntary confinement of anybody in psychiatric institutions. Local officials who are zealous in enforcing the one-child family planning policy are often mindful about revenues from fines that they could collect from those they accused of violation of the birth quotas. Another area of rights violations often in the news is land seizure, forced eviction, and demolition of housing. Why are the commercial developers so emboldened and blatant in using violence and the police tend to look the other way or join them? The developers have the backing of government officials, who receive huge kickbacks when they issue permits to developers to grab land from farmers or demolish urban housing.

What about seeking justice and legal remedies through the court? The Chinese judiciary has no independence from the Party and the government. An office known as the "Political and Legal Committee" presides over the court, interfering in court proceedings and dictating the verdicts in important cases, such as cases involving dissidents, or whistleblowers who disclosed corruption of powerful officials, or journalists who reported on polluting factories that are cash cows for government officials.

Now I turn to the question of why the Xi Jinping government is staging a crackdown on citizens who simply acted upon Xi Jinping's own call to fight corruption. The first point, and a very basic one, that I want to make is that, in the lack of an accountable and representative government, without a rule of law, a free press, or a robust civil society, no government can clean up corruption. This simple lesson has been tested many times in modern Chinese history—ever since Chairman Mao, Chinese leaders for several generations have had their own noisy campaigns against corruption in the CCP [Chinese Communist Party] and the government. In fact, the Party has developed an elaborate extrajudicial system to punish and discipline CCP members and officials. The system, known as *shuanggui,* is complete with detention cells and interrogation chambers, where torture and mistreatment of fallen leaders are known to be rampant. You can't say they didn't try. But corruption has only become worse today.

So it's not surprising that President Xi Jinping is again making anticorruption a priority of his new leadership. The new leaders worry that corruption is eroding any remaining legitimacy that the CCP still has. A decade ago, one might be able to argue that the CCP struck a deal with the population: People were allowed to make money, get rich, as long as they don't challenge the CCP's monopoly of power; and this was said to be a sort of social contract. But today, the middle classes find that they got a lousy deal: They don't just want to make money, they want health, clean air, fair share of their work, and they want to protect what they earned and have some say in decisions that affect them. But the political system does not allow them access to information and the decision-making process. And corrupt officials rob them of what they consider rightfully belonging to them. Press censorship and political interference in the judicial system obstruct them from seeking remedies. Growing social conflicts must have made the ruling elite feel very insecure. Xi Jinping's anticorruption campaign, along with some of the small concessions to popular demands, such as those rolled out last week by the CCP Central Committee, is intended to ease the crisis of the CCP's legitimacy and prolong its rule. It is to placate popular anger—showing the people that "we are on your side and we too want to end corruption."

Yet, Xi Jinping, with his pedigree as princeling of a revolutionary elder, may have more at stake than Jiang Zemin and Hu Jintao in preventing the collapse of the political system under his watch, though he might try to patch up some cracks and adopt small fixes. Unless fundamental reform of the political system takes place, however, Xi Jinping's anticorruption campaign, that is said to go after "flies and tigers," will never succeed beyond "killing a few chickens to frighten the monkeys." So far, the campaign has only been instrumental in getting rid of political rivals like Bo Xilai.

The point I am trying to make is that it is inevitable that the Xi leadership is presiding over a crackdown on civil society activists who campaigned against corruption. Since last March, the government has criminalized journalists and microbloggers for exposing corruption. And police have criminally detained several dozens of activists in Beijing and the provinces. The activists face criminal charges for publicly calling on the country's 200-plus top leaders to disclose their personal wealth. Their alleged crimes include "inciting subversion," "unlawful assembly," and "gathering a crowd to disrupt public order." Among those detained are the legal scholar and activist, Xu Zhiyong, and a few other democracy activists like Zhao Changqing, and human rights lawyers like Ding Jiaxi, who were key members of the "New Citizens' Movement."

So here is the key to solve our puzzle: Both the leaders and the civil society activists understand that genuine efforts to clean up corruption must take aim at fundamentally changing the one-party-ruled authoritarian system. But Xi Jinping wants to protect the system and his own power, by taking out a few corrupt officials and political rivals, while Xu Zhiyong and his colleagues want to change the system and bring democratic and rule-of-law reforms by starting with tackling official corruption.

There was an illuminating exchange between Xu Zhiyong and the police interrogators. The interrogators tried to get him to acknowledge that the Party was heading in the right direction. Xu conceded that fighting corruption is good, but insisted that "the problem is the system." It is impossible to end corruption, he said, while maintaining a system in which all the powers are controlled by one political party—including the press, the courts, the schools, and the economy.

The Chinese leaders no doubt could see Xu's point. But they cannot end the one-party rule; their power would perish with it. To maintain their power, they must crush the citizen-led anticorruption campaign and jail its leading activists.

The swiftness and harshness of this crackdown is perhaps a good measure of the strength of Chinese civil society activism. Organized public actions were rare even a few years ago, and the government now regards activists like Xu Zhiyong as a serious threat. Xu's police interrogators told him that they watched his "New Citizens' Movement" swell to several thousand members in just a few months. "If we do not put a stop to this immediately, it will bring chaos and instability all over the country," they said. But the Chinese leaders may want to think about this: Whether imprisoning and silencing anticorruption activists can help fight corruption, quiet public anger, and ultimately, whether more repression can prolong the Party's rule. Thank you.

Mr. LIU. Thank you.

Dr. Wedeman?

STATEMENT OF ANDREW WEDEMAN, PROFESSOR, DEPARTMENT OF POLITICAL SCIENCE, GEORGIA STATE UNIVERSITY

Mr. WEDEMAN. Well, I have the advantage of going third, so I can respond to the people who came before me. Joe Fewsmith suggested at the beginning of this talk that this current campaign was perhaps the most serious and sustained we had seen in several decades and that it might well have teeth, but then toward the end of his talk he had talked himself off that position to a similar position of Li Xiaorong, basically to say perhaps this is just another iteration of the same old song and dance.

You can go back to Hu Yaobang, you can go back to Jiang Zemin, you can go to Hu Jintao. They have all said the same thing: If we don't fight corruption it will kill the Party. Of course, wags in China then go on to say, and if they fight corruption it will certainly kill the Party.

There is a fundamental question here that we confront in the wake of the Bo Xilai and the more recent scandals, and that is, is corruption worse in China today than it was in the past? It is a very difficult question to answer because we actually can't figure out what the actual level of corruption is in China.

All we've got are two very imperfect measures. We've got something I call the revealed rate of corruption, which is quite simply the body count: How many people are indicted, how many people are tried, how many people are sent to prison?

The other measure is the one that Transparency International and others have created. I call it the perceived level of corruption.

It's the best guess of experts, multiple experts, done in a scientific poll, so on and so forth, but it's basically a guess.

And where do you think they get their guess? From the body count. So what does the body count tell us? Actually, there are three different body counts. There's the body count of the people that get investigated by the Party, there's the body count of people who get indicted by the Supreme People's Procuratorate, and there's the body count of people who are tried and convicted in the People's Court.

The Party is the first step in the process. The Party also is one of the least willing to share their data, so the data we have on the Party is relatively imperfect. Probably the most systematic data we have is from the procuratorate, and essentially what we have is the number of people indicted—in Chinese terms, the cases filed—every year.

Well, for the past decade it's been about 35,000. It has not gone up significantly, it has not gone down. It varies a little bit each year. My projection for this year, it's going to be as the Chinese say "*cha bu duo*," it'll be about the same as the year before, about 34,000. Of those 34,000, 90-plus percent are rank-and-file officials. About 2,200, 2,300 are people who hold leadership positions at the county and departmental level, about 200 are at the municipal and bureau level.

Somewhere between 5 and 10 are at the provincial or ministerial level. The numbers have not changed. The numbers that we're looking at for the current campaign, I think I've got eight at the most senior level versus five last year. Does that mean that this is a significant gain? Yes? Maybe? I can't tell. I think actually the number to really look at is the mid-level number, and we won't know that until we get the official report.

So right now it doesn't look like, in fact, things actually have gotten worse. We've had all these great scandals, right? Bo Xilai, the Minister of Railways, et cetera. The problem is that when you look at a corruption case, there are two important dates. There's the stop date, which is the date they get arrested, detained, et cetera, and that's an interesting measure of changes in enforcement.

If we look at the stop date it doesn't look like it has moved very much. In other words, they are arresting about as many people each year this year as they were last year and the year before, et cetera.

The more important date, if we're really interested in the question "is corruption getting worse," is the start date. If you go back and you look at the major cases that have been revealed in this campaign, they're not new cases, they're old cases.

Bo Xilai's case began in 1994, 20 years ago. That's when he became corrupt. In 2012, he stopped being corrupt when he was detained, imprisoned, et cetera. So we turn around and we say, well, is corruption worse under Xi Jinping? Well, we would have to know an awful lot of data about start dates, yet what we have mostly is stop dates. So that complicates the analysis.

The second area that I want to comment on, is when you look at a corruption campaign in one level, as Li Xiaorong says, it is an exercise in taking out your political rivals. It is an opportunity to go after people. But a campaign operates on multiple different levels. On one level it is political, and I will say a little bit more about the politics of this particular one.

The other part of it is, it's an exercise in public relations. You get a scandal, you get Bo Xilai with the dead Englishman in the out-of-the-way Chongqing hotel, tales of arsenic and old lace, et cetera, you have got to respond to it and you have got to, as Li Xiaorong says, you have got to kill some chickens or you have got to get some tiger pelts.

So they'll take out some senior level people not purely for political reasons, but for PR reasons. They need to go out and get some people to show that they're really ready to fight corruption, at least to convince the people, if in fact I think as Joe ended up suggesting, they probably really aren't making any real headway.

The other thing is, this particular anticorruption campaign has a feature that the ones in the past did not. Early on, even before Xi got into office, the Internet was driving part of this campaign. There were these numerous exposures, some of them having to do with excess property, some with mistresses, some with mistresses and property, expensive watches, and so on and so forth. That drove the campaign at the lower levels because these are mostly targeting officials who were in the public view. So there's that level. There's also the political level.

I started looking at the cases, and if you pick up the document I dropped off and I think it's available out front, I started looking at cases that would attach to Zhou Yongkang, the former head of the Politics and Law Commission of the Central Committee. It is astounding how many people are connected to—how many of the cases that we are tracking now track back to him. So there's a clearly political element to the campaign. Yes, Xi Jinping is taking out political rivals. He seems to be taking out an awful lot of them. Now, I don't think he's going to go after Zhou.

You look at Zhou, you track him back to Zeng Qinghong, who tracks back to the old Shanghai gang, and before you know it you're suddenly looking at the grand old man of Chinese politics Jiang Zemin. If you are Xi Jinping trying to consolidate your position as the new General Secretary, my advice to you as a political advisor is, do not take on Jiang Zemin. So, do not take out Zhou Yongkang, take out a lot of people around him.

The final thing I will point out about this campaign is it continues to intensify a drive that began in about 2006, which is targeting corruption within the business sector. It is targeting two parts of that, both within the state-owned sector, which Professor Chow will talk about, but also within the private sector as well.

One of the things the Chinese are beginning to realize, and the United States realized in the mid-1970s, is if you're going to fight corruption you can't just fight official corruption because official corruption is the supply side. You have to fight the demand side as well. Businessmen—I know lots of businessmen. I know honest ones and I know some dishonest ones.

A bribe is just a cost if you can get away with it. Often it is very profitable. You are not going to really make real headway on corruption among officials unless you start going after the people who pay the bribes, as well as the people who take the bribes.

One of the features of this campaign that I have really been struck by is how many of the people getting taken out are on the business side. So the final question I have about the campaign is, how far are they going to go in attacking business corruption? All that said, I think the campaign is on its way out. I think we are at the near end of it. These are things you only want to fight so long. You want to kill some chickens, you want to get some tiger pelts, but you don't want to push it too far. So I think we're on the verge of seeing it begin to wind down, and I will close there.

Mr. LIU. Thank you very much, Dr. Wedeman.

Our last speaker, Professor Chow.

[The prepared statement of Mr. Wedeman appears in the appendix.]

STATEMENT OF DANIEL CHOW, PROFESSOR OF INTERNATIONAL LAW, OHIO STATE UNIVERSITY, MORITZ COLLEGE OF LAW

Mr. CHOW. I am going to focus on the recent crackdown on commercial bribery, the role of state-owned enterprises in commercial bribery, and the impact of these anticorruption campaigns on U.S.-based multinational companies doing business in China.

So, now, I am a lawyer so some of this is going to be a little bit legal, so I am warning you in advance. So as I see it, there are two recent developments which pose threats to U.S.-based multinational companies doing business in China.

The first, is the recent emphasis, as Professor Wedeman alluded to, on cracking down on commercial bribery. So first and foremost, let's get this out of the way. What is commercial bribery? Commercial bribery—I'm just going to simplify it a little bit. In my paper it's going to be a little bit more elaborate. But commercial bribery occurs when a company, a business, pays a bribe in order to get business. That's commercial bribery.

So a company pays a bribe, perhaps, to another company to get business or it pays a bribe to a government official to get business. That is commercial bribery, it is when a company pays a bribe for the purpose of getting business.

Distinguish that from, say, government graft, government corruption. I will give you an example. Suppose that a state-owned oil company borrows hundreds of millions of dollars from a state-owned bank in order to buy an oil well overseas and they overstate the price of the oil well by $100 million.

So what they do, is they get the loan, they buy the oil well, and they keep $100 million. Now, that is not commercial bribery, that is graft. That is official corruption, so that is not what I am referring to. I am referring to, now, when a company gives a bribe to get business.

Now, I'm going to focus on company-to-company bribes as opposed to company-to-government official bribes, and I'm going to focus on company-to-company bribes, or business-to-business bribes because, on the one end of the transaction is often a multinational company that is giving the bribe and on the receiving end of the bribe is often a state-owned enterprise that is receiving the bribe and will give the multinational some business.

Now, since I mentioned state-owned enterprise, I suppose now we need to make sure we know what a state-owned enterprise is, and I'm going to give you a rather simple, straightforward definition here. That is, a business entity which has been established by the central or the local government and which is subject to supervision by the government or by the Communist Party.

Now, supervision could be because there is a government bureau that supervises the state-owned enterprise, and in addition the Communist Party will place key officials within the state-owned enterprise to make sure they control it.

Now, I want to mention so that we are all clear that today there are over 200,000 state-owned enterprises. It depends on how you count them, and there is some disagreement, but I would say there's certainly at least 120,000, and some people, the law firms, say that there are 200,000. They dominate in all core industries in China.

So what do I mean by that? Petroleum, banking, telecommunications, transportation, auto, electric supply, oil and gas, electronics, chemicals. All of the core industries are dominated by state-owned enterprises, which means what? It means that the Communist Party controls the core economic sectors of China.

Now, in addition to this recent emphasis on cracking down on commercial bribery, I want to mention that there is a new interpretation issued by the Supreme People's Court, together with the Supreme People's Procuratorate, about a year ago which now emphasizes enforcement against the payor of the bribe, whereas emphasis in the past has been on the recipient, or the payee, of the bribe.

Now, I think this is consistent with the crackdown on commercial bribery, because when you focus on the payor of the bribe, that is often a multinational company. Now, just think about it for a second. There are two choke points when it comes to bribery. One, is you can go after the bribe taker or you can go after the bribe giver. If you go after the bribe taker you are going to implicate government officials. You may implicate Party officials.

But if you go after the bribe giver, you are going after GlaxoSmithKline, you are going after Eli Lilly, you are going after the multinational companies and you are going to score a lot of political points and it is going to have a lot of symbolic impact.

So I think these two developments, the emphasis on commercial bribery, the focus on the payor of the bribe, create significant risks for U.S.-based multinationals doing business in China. But the risk that is created for the U.S.-based multinationals is not prosecution under Chinese law, it is prosecution under U.S. law under a law called the Foreign Corrupt Practices Act, which prohibits U.S. companies from paying bribes to foreign officials—this is a technical term, foreign officials—in order to obtain or retain business.

Now, I am going to put the risks under the Foreign Corrupt Practices Act, due to the new emphasis on commercial bribery, into three categories, all involving state-owned enterprise. First, many multinational businesses sell their products to state-owned enterprises.

State-owned enterprises are known to be highly corrupt. This is common knowledge in China and it is common for state-owned enterprises both to make and receive bribes in doing business. Now, under the Department of Justice interpretation of the Foreign Corrupt Practice Act, every employee of a state-owned enterprise is deemed to be a foreign official, from the most highest ranking to the lowest ranking clerical employee.

So what is a very common scenario, which I am going to describe in a second, is going to create problems under the Foreign Corrupt Practices Act for multinational companies. Suppose a sales agent in a multinational company gives a kickback, a bribe, to a purchasing agent, which is a low-level employee in a state-owned enterprise to induce that purchasing agent to buy, say, chemicals or to, say, buy a radiation detector—a real case—from the multinational's China business entity.

Although the purchasing agent is deemed to be of the state-owned enterprise, is deemed to be a low-level employee, the Department of Justice could consider the employee to be a foreign official and could consider the payment of the kickback to be a bribe given to a foreign official in order to obtain business to complete the sale.

That would be a violation of the Foreign Corrupt Practices Act and, in my opinion, with the crackdown on commercial bribery by China, more of these transactions will come to light, leading to more investigations under the Foreign Corrupt Practices Act by the Department of Justice.

The Department of Justice monitors the media in China. They do not know about these kickback schemes. But if the Chinese authorities go after somebody, it gets in the media and the next day the Department of Justice contacts the U.S. company and demands an explanation.

Now, of the 12 Foreign Corrupt Practices actions filed last year by the Department of Justice, 5 of them involved China, all of them in one sector, the healthcare sector. China has announced crackdowns on commercial bribery involving pharmaceutical companies. GlaxoSmithKline, which is based in England, has been the subject of a crackdown and they are the payor of the bribe.

GlaxoSmithKline could well be investigated under the Foreign Corrupt Practices Act. It is a British company, but they issue securities on the New York Stock Exchange, which means that they qualify as an issuer under the Foreign Corrupt Practices Act as is thus subject to the anti-bribery, as well as the books and records provisions.

China has now announced that it is going to go after 60 pharmaceutical companies and investigate these companies for illegal payments, again, the emphasis on the commercial nature of the payment to get business and the emphasis on the payor. The pharmaceutical companies give kickbacks to doctors so that the doctors can prescribe medicines in China. Everybody in China knows this.

The second category of risk is that multinational companies doing business in China deal with state-owned enterprises all the time and state-owned enterprises have a pervasive culture of what I call petty corruption, meaning that when multinational companies deal with procurement issues, that is, selling to state-owned enterprises, the state-owned enterprise employees will demand gifts.

The Foreign Corrupt Practices Act prohibits the giving of "anything of value," so a job for a son, a job for a daughter, an internship for a son, that is something that would be a possible violation of the Foreign Corrupt Practices Act.

Kickbacks in China demanded by state-owned enterprises [SOEs] are very common. They happen every single day. This type of petty corruption is tolerated by many people in China just as a cost of doing business.

The third category of risk that I see for multinational companies as a result of these recent developments is that many multinationals must deal with third parties in China. Multinational companies—and this I think is one of the greatest areas of exposure.

So for example, a multinational company doing business in China might form a joint venture [JV] with a local Chinese company, often the state-owned enterprise. In fact, certain industries are required by law for the multinational to form a JV.

The multinational cannot go it alone in certain industries. So you form your joint venture with the state-owned enterprise as your local partner and the state-owned enterprise has been used to giving bribes for years.

Now it is your joint venture partner and they continue to give bribes. When they give bribes, the multinational company is deemed to be liable for the actions of the joint venture, right, because that is your joint venture, it is in China, it is your agent, you are liable under the Foreign Corrupt Practices Act for the actions of the local partner.

Finally, I want to say that multinational companies deal with so-called consultants, lawyers, public relations people, distributors all the time and a lot of these third parties pass through bribes. You get a bill from the third party consultant, a miscellaneous expense for $10,000. Now, what is that? Well, that is often going to be a bribe. That is something that many multinationals have to face, and that is dealing with third parties.

So the crackdown on commercial bribery, I think, will create higher exposures for U.S.-based multinational companies doing business in China, not under Chinese law, because Chinese authorities really have no interest in destroying or really hurting GlaxoSmithKline. That's like cutting off your nose to spite your face. It is a big, huge company, earns tremendous revenues. They want to teach them a lesson but they do not really want to hurt them. However, under the Foreign Corrupt Practices Act the penalties can be extremely severe and the crackdown by China could bring the attention of the Department of Justice [DOJ] to Foreign Corrupt Practices Act cases.

I am just going to close with one point, and that is that in my opinion this crackdown on corruption involving state-owned enterprises, that really isn't going to change anything if there isn't going to be any fundamental reform of state-owned enterprises. The issue in state-owned enterprises is that they enjoy monopoly power, monopoly power over something like petroleum involving billions of dollars.

You have an official who makes—some of the top officials now actually make quite a bit of money, over $100,000, $500,000, maybe

$1 million. But they look around and they know they control hundreds of millions of dollars, so it's the monopoly power, the relatively low salaries of executives in state-owned enterprises which creates what appears to be an irresistible temptation to engage in commercial bribery.

Thank you.

[The prepared statement of Mr. Chow appears in the appendix.]

Mr. LIU. Thank you very much, Professor Chow.

Thank you to all of our panelists for an extremely informative presentation covering various aspects of this very important issue. I wanted to allow some time for some questions. I know our staff have a few questions, and then we can open it up to the audience.

I believe Anna Brettell from our staff, our Senior Advisor, has a question.

Ms. BRETTELL. Yes, I have a question. Since 2010, Party and government organizations have issued regulations regarding the disclosure of officials' assets or the assets of their families, as well as information regarding family members who had gone abroad.

Since the third plenum, there have been a couple of news articles with commentary by people who thought that Chinese officials should disclose their assets to the public, because the previous regulations just required officials to disclose their assets to the Party or to the organization within which they work.

Do you think that there may be some regulations coming down the pike that would require certain officials, and also leaders of SOEs, to disclose their assets to the public? Anybody is free to answer.

Mr. FEWSMITH. It is really hard to imagine, it really is. This has been talked about in China for several years and we do not see anything on the public disclosure side. I guess I would have to be very surprised if you had anything serious. Of course, you could put assets under the name of relatives or something like that and get around such regulations, but I just find it hard to believe that you'll see anything serious in this regard. Andrew would like to disagree.

Mr. WEDEMAN. No, actually, I fully agree. Taiwan actually implemented an assets disclosure law back in the 1990s and the Lifa Yuan, the parliament, was under a lot of pressure to do this. So they passed a sweeping law: All government officials must disclose their assets.

But they did something very interesting. They then failed to fund an agency to read the forms. They gave them enough money to check off that the form was submitted, but nobody bothered to go through the form and actually check out if it was honest.

I looked at hundreds of these. It was amazing. Poor Taiwanese politicians and officials had no money in the bank, because you could get a bank account under any name, and of course if there was no one to check who those accounts belonged to, you didn't have to list it.

I don't know what the status of that is at this point, but as long as you require officials to disclose assets and you don't have public or governmental auditing of those disclosures, they're basically meaningless. Given that in the past few weeks there have been new regulations on the disclosure of things that had been on the

Internet, like property records, I see them actually going the opposite direction to try and keep whatever—anything that is disclosed will be a state secret in order to protect the guilty.

Ms. BRETTELL. I have another quick question. Daniel Chow, you started talking about how China was changing its focus of corruption investigations, going after the bribers instead of the receivers of the bribe. Do you see this as part of a trend where Chinese officials are targeting international or multinational companies [MNCs] or do you think that the Chinese officials are just going after corruption anywhere it rears its head?

I read one article where someone argued that Chinese officials are not intentionally going after multinational companies, but that they are targeting these companies first as a trial—and that these efforts are for PR value. Do you have any thoughts on that?

Mr. CHOW. Yes. Well, I think that as I mentioned, when you think about it, there are two choke points when you deal with bribery. One is the recipient, to go after the recipient, and the other is to go after the giver of the bribe.

Now, China has been focused almost entirely on the recipient of the bribe, but in 2012, in December 2012, is when the Supreme People's Court and the Supreme People's Procuratorate passed a new law in which they said that we're going to focus on the giver, or the payor, of the bribe. The remedies are actually quite serious and they talk about the possibility of criminal liability for certain bribes.

Now, are they targeting or going unfairly after multinationals? Well, when you say "unfairly," multinationals give bribes. I mean, they have been doing that for a long time because everybody says that this is how you have to do business. So in my opinion they do want to make examples of the multinationals and they're going after the multinationals.

However, I do not think they really want to hurt the multinationals. What they do want, is they want to investigate a few people, maybe give them a jail sentence here or there, but they have no interest, in my opinion, in really harming the multinationals and taking away their business license.

So I think they do want to go after the multinationals because people are so angry about corruption. This is an area that they have not focused on until recently, but in my opinion it is largely symbolic. I do not think that they are really out to hurt, shut down GlaxoSmithKline, shut down Eli Lilly. I don't think they're trying to do that. I think they're trying to make a symbolic point.

Mr. WEDEMAN. They've actually been cracking down on commercial bribery since 2006. Lo and behold, in 2006 when they introduced the category, 80 percent of bribery cases were suddenly commercial bribery. They have obviously been prosecuting these cases for a long time, and my recollection is the original laws banning the paying of bribes for commercial purposes date to the mid-1990s, but it was not until 2006 that they started enforcing it.

I think actually part of the reason why they're going after the MNCs is they saw all the cases being prosecuted by DOJ, and they said, "Well, gee, if DOJ is catching all these people then maybe we should go after them, too." I agree with you that there is a political element in the current atmosphere, striking at foreign bribes and payoffs has political advantages.

Mr. PROTIC. I have a question. Have Chinese journalists tried to take on corruption, and what have been the results?

Ms. LI. That question requires a long answer, but I think many Chinese journalists are taking on corruption, and obviously they are also taking great personal risk for doing that. There have been quite a number of cases in recent months of journalists or citizen journalists including bloggers or Internet commentators who have been prosecuted for exposing official corruption. What is happening here is that the officials who are being personally vindicated when these reporters disclosed their involvement in corruption would take revenge and try to cover up themselves by using their power to silence or criminalize the reporters. These officials would turn the tables around and accuse the journalists of using bribery to get the scoop, for example, or using the information for some illicit purposes.

So at the end of the day, it's the journalists who reported on corruption who might lose their jobs or serve jail time. But going after official corruption seems to be one of the areas where the younger generation of journalists and cyber commentators are willing to take the risk and they are doing some inventive investigative journalism in this area.

Mr. LIU. Thank you. I just had one more question, I think, from our side of the table and then I wanted to open it up to the general public. But we have some U.S. policymakers in the audience, Hill staff, and I wanted to get your thoughts on how U.S. policymakers should be thinking about this issue, whether we should be in any ways supporting the Chinese leadership's campaign against corruption, given the fact that many of you have expressed skepticism regarding it and whether it is more for PR purposes. How should U.S. policymakers here on the Hill and in the U.S. Government be thinking about this issue, and how should they address it with the Chinese? Any of you?

Mr. FEWSMITH. I'm not sure. I haven't really thought this one through, but it seems to me this one might be one where the U.S. Government might actually want to be a bit more restrained. Corruption doesn't—except if they are systematically going after U.S. companies, that's one thing, if there's evidence of that sort of thing.

But if they're trying to crack down on their own corruption, that's a good thing. If they fail in their campaign, well, that is a bad thing for China, for the Chinese Government, for the Chinese people. But I just can't see points of pressure, that it would be particularly—there are a lot bigger fish to fry than their own internal problems.

Mr. CHOW. I do want to say that the U.S. Government is cooperating with China and they are working together on implementing the UN Convention Against Bribery, which is different from what I've been talking about, the Foreign Corrupt Practices Act, or the U.K. Bribery Act, because the UN Convention allows for asset recovery, which means that you can recover the assets which have been illegally obtained.

A lot of those assets have made their way to the United States as corrupt officials have bought real estate in the United States, and so the United States is working with the Chinese Government to recover some of those assets and maybe extradite some of these corrupt officials who think, I can get rich in China and I can retire to America. So there is some cooperation there. I certainly think that there should be further cooperation between the United States and China on these issues.

Mr. WEDEMAN. I agree with Professor Chow. What I'm told, though, is the problem isn't that the United States isn't willing to go after assets and go for extradition, the Chinese side won't provide sufficient evidence to get the United States to seize assets and extradite people because they don't want to reveal the internal documents from their investigation.

So what I was told by an agency of the U.S. Government, somebody who worked for it, they know that there are corrupt officials hiding here. They know that there is dirty money, but the Chinese will not go after it. It is fascinating to me that the Chinese have made no effort, as far as I know, to go after Bo Guagua, who is paying $50,000 a year to attend Columbia University and he has no income. His father is in jail, his mother is in jail. All of their assets have been seized. Where is he getting the money? I mean, the U.S. IRS could go after him, right? Somebody is paying his bills.

Mr. CHOW. This must have been part of the deal they struck, right, when they said we'll give you a life sentence and so forth. It was part of the deal, we're not going to go after your son. You can criticize various people in your trial. Maybe that was part of the deal.

Mr. WEDEMAN. Perhaps. But that doesn't mean the United States couldn't go after him for tax evasion, right?

Mr. CHOW. That's true.

Ms. LI. For U.S. lawmakers, the Chinese leaders' anticorruption slogan, whether it is for PR, or as a political tool to get rid of political rivals, could be an entry point to start a conversation about the systemic problems. The conversation could, for example, start with the point that it is good that the Chinese leaders said they wanted to get rid of corruption; now here are some of the changes that need to be made or measures to be taken, which we have learned are necessary to cleaning up government; and our experiences told us that there should be government transparency and power must be checked and balanced, et cetera.

So a conversation that begins with anticorruption can lead to discussions of some of the structural problems. As Professor Fewsmith pointed out, the root of corruption is really in the system, the political structure, which is ultimately responsible for the continuing existence of incentives for abusing power, loopholes for evading accountability, et cetera.

Vice President Joe Biden is going to China soon. We know that he had a nice rapport with President Xi Jinping, so maybe he could start the conversation with Xi: If you're serious about cleaning up corruption, look, here are some fundamental changes to make in order to deal with some of the root problems.

Mr. FEWSMITH. But I don't think that China has the least bit of interest in changing the system. In fact, I might hazard a guess that it has less interest in it now than it did 10 years ago.

Ms. LI. That is what I said.

Mr. LIU. All right. Thank you. Oh, sorry. Go ahead.

Mr. WEDEMAN. They're not unaware of how the United States went out and combated corruption. You go to Chinese universities, they have departments of Public Administration. They don't have political science departments, by and large. That is because that is the way we did it, we did it through civil service reform with resisting political reform to a certain extent. When did the era of machine politics end? The 1970s in Chicago? Or perhaps not, if you look at Southern California politics.

So I think on a technical level, Chinese scholars are aware of what should be done. But I would agree with Joe, the one thing you don't want to give up is the monopoly on political power held by the Communist Party. Until you get rid of that, you don't break the powers of the Party secretaries, you don't eliminate their ability to buy and sell offices, seize land, skim off from public works, et cetera, et cetera.

Mr. CHOW. Yes. Well, the committee that investigates discipline, which is another word for corruption, is controlled by the Communist Party, so the Party is investigating itself. So, of course, there is going to be a limit on what is going to happen in this campaign and how far up they will go. They're not going to go very far up.

Mr. LIU. I want to give us the last 15 minutes for the audience to be able to ask any questions they may have for our excellent group of panelists. If you want to raise your hand. We have two microphones, one on this side of the stage and the other in the back there. This is being webcast and there will be a transcript, so you don't have to introduce yourself or give your affiliation. If you just want to ask a question, you are welcome to do so. Yes, go for it.

PARTICIPANT. I do have a technical question about how to measure corruption in China. You mentioned the [inaudible] measure. It seems to me this measure is pointless or useless. The reason is simple. Because although you have official statistics about how many officials are prosecuted or convicted every year, you just don't have another important statistic, that is how many officials are there in China. For example, about—the provincial-level corruption. You just don't know how many provincial officials are there in China. For example, you may offer a guess of several thousand or tens of thousands, but there is no public figures there. So I don't see why you count every year how many provincial officials are prosecuted because you don't know the total number. If you don't know the total number, what is the point to count how many are investigated every year? That's the question. Thanks.

Mr. WEDEMAN. I don't think you're right. I think we do know the number. We do.

PARTICIPANT. Really? Okay. So how many?

Mr. WEDEMAN. I haven't looked it up recently, but we probably do know. The percentage is obviously quite low in the number of people being prosecuted. The second reason why you look at the number, is you want to look at the number compared to the year before. I mean, that's an indicator of something. Yes, we don't know what percentage of officials are corrupt. We don't know that anywhere. I don't even want to suggest that perhaps some Members of the Congress are on the take, or bureaucracy. The only way we know is when they get caught. There is no way to know it.

So the thing is, the objection that the data are no good, the alternative is, well, I do not want to look at hard data, I just want to make up my own opinion. So I think you've got to pay attention to the data. When you look at those numbers, basically I look at them and what they tell me is, in statistical terms, nothing has happened. They go up, they go down. I can't tell if it means anything, can't tell if it means nothing at all. So yes, you do. I mean, you can't just throw the numbers out because they're not perfect because it's the only data you have.

Mr. FEWSMITH. You do actually have data on the size of the [inaudible] every year will say so many people were convicted and the amounts are going up year by year. So we do have some data.

PARTICIPANT. But you don't have the percentage.

Mr. FEWSMITH. No, no. But that would be so small.

Mr. LIU. Yes, the gentleman here in the third row.

MICHAEL. Hello. Michael is my name. Two questions. Perhaps you've touched on them, but I didn't hear it. One of them concerns corruption or bribery in the medical profession. You had mentioned the public health sector.

And the second, is in the military. I understand that there is considerable bribery, including the purchasing of ranks. But I wonder if the panel would care to venture into either of those two minefields, the medical or the military.

Mr. CHOW. Well, let me just talk about, right now, that there is an ongoing emphasis on commercial bribery in the pharmaceutical sector so that we have 60—China just recently announced that they are going to start investigating 60 pharmaceutical companies which have been involved in giving kickbacks to doctors who prescribe their medications.

It's a sophisticated scheme which involves the use of travel agencies. So you set up a travel agency or you work with a travel agency and you submit to the travel agency false expense documents, or excuse me, the travel agency supplies those to you. You take them to your company and you get reimbursed. That's the money you get to give to the doctors for the kickbacks.

The other thing that has happened is that doctors have been given trips to resort locations. You know, you get to go to Macau, for example, for the weekend for a medical conference and nothing happens except you play golf. So that is something that China is focused on.

So actually, China is focused on three areas right now. Health care is a focus, banking is a focus because there is so much money there, and then real estate development is also a focus because the real estate speculation is so tremendous. So that's what's been going on in the pharmaceutical sector.

So GlaxoSmithKline is currently being investigated. Four executives have been detained. Pfizer has been investigated by the Justice Department and they have reached a settlement with the Justice Department. Eli Lilly has been investigated. So that's one area in which there is quite a bit of activity that is going on in China.

MICHAEL. I meant to include the bribery that citizens throughout China have to pay in order to get access to medical care. Somebody needs surgery, you can't get that surgery unless the bribe reaches stage X.

Mr. CHOW. Well, also if you go to a hospital in China you know you're not going to get good treatment unless you give the doctor a red envelope. So nothing is being done about that as far as I know, because that involves just ordinary people. So as far as I know, that continues to go on.

Mr. WEDEMAN. Corruption among the military is the black hole of information in China. The military controls its investigations internally. We see nothing, we hear nothing, except occasionally there is a very small number of cases. But one has to assume that there's quite a bit more.

You can't be building up the military at the rate that they are building it up without a lot of corruption. Military procurement programs worldwide are infamous for $600 toilets, to go back to the 1980s in the United States. The military also controls a great deal of real estate, and that can be parlayed into some very lucrative deals. The fact that there are lucrative opportunities means that it is lucrative to buy and sell ranks. But how much, who, where, when? Good luck on that.

MICHAEL. And no indication that the Party is looking?

Mr. WEDEMAN. The Party says it's cracking down on it, but the military handles it internally and it does not make Liberation Daily headlines.

Mr. LIU. The gentleman back here.

PARTICIPANT. I'm glad this gentleman asked about the corruption in the military and medical. I think to talk about that we have to mention the organ harvesting that has happened in the last decade in China. There has been more and more evidence showing that this killing by demand has been happening there. This is called, by a professor in Biomedics at New York University, killing by demand. Probably tens of thousands of Falun Gong practitioners have been killed and organs have been sold for a huge profit. So that's my comment.

I do have a question to the panel. Recently, the Chinese Communist Party has announced the closing of labor camps. A lot of the people applauded that. But actually from the victims that we know in China, the persecution of a lot of people, especially Falun Gong practitioners, has not been lessened at all. They simply change the forms of the persecution.

For example, they changed the signs at the labor camps from The Center of Reeducation Through Labor to Legal Education Center, or they simply directly transported those people from labor camps to existing Legal Education Centers, or they put more people through a show trial to give them prison sentences. So actually the persecution has been even intensified.

Because we talk about corruption, I think it has to do with the legal system. If the legal system simply cannot protect the basic human rights of the people, we certainly cannot expect that to prevent the corruption from happening.

So my question to the panel is, what do you think would be the effective way to pressure the Chinese Communist regime to stop the religious persecution there, especially the persecution of the largest victim group, Falun Gong? Thank you.

Ms. LI. It's very interesting that you pointed out that the to-be-abolished reeducation through labor [RTL] camps are just a matter of changing names. I think that is one of the dangers here because we know, since early this year, several provinces announced that they would phase out the use of RTL. As far as we could see, there have been fewer cases involving people being sent to RTL since early 2013.

One obvious question to ask is: Where have those taken away by police been detained? The number of people being detained or deprived of their freedoms has not seemed to go down. There have been reports of petitioners, practitioners of Falun Gong, activists being detained. So they must have been kept somewhere other than the RTL.

One thing we should watch closely is, while RTL may be abolished, it might be quietly replaced by other extrajudicial detention facilities, including what you mention as legal education centers, "black jails," which is just any facility turned into makeshift detention cells by authorities to lock up people without any judicial oversight. It could be government offices, hotels, official guest houses, et cetera.

The Chinese Communist Party Central Committee Third Plenum announced last month in its decision, under Article 34, that RTL will be abolished. It also announced that the government will put out a draft law authorizing another system of punishment called Illegal Behavior Education and Correction. This is an interesting development, but one has to watch very carefully what is shaping up as a replacement for RTL. Supposedly, those who are minor criminals should instead be sent to those correction centers. Such correction is supposed to be conducted in what the decision called "communities."

What do they mean by "community?" Here lies another potential problem. The existing so-called "legal study classes," the "black jails," are handled by local officials. Is that what the government means by "community correction centers?" Who is going to be supervising those "community correction centers" operated by local officials? What judicial procedure is going to be put in place to oversee the trials and the verdicts of those to be sent to "community correction centers?" In other words, will the decision go through court procedures or be decided by local officials or police, like under the RTL system? These are some of the interesting things to watch. When it comes to depriving liberty, involving human rights questions, how are such decisions going to made and overseen? What will authorities do with those whom they previously would send to RTL?

This year, we have seen that when police detain petitioners, or practitioners of Falun Gong, or rights activists, who would previously have been sent to RTL, police have put them either under criminal detention, charged with various, often trumped-up crimes, such as "gathering a crowd to disrupt public order," or "creating trouble," a crime that is like a sack in which police could practically put in anything. It seems that, in the place of RTL, authorities have increased the use of the criminal system.

We also observed an interesting reversal of the course of prohibiting "black jails." A couple of years ago, the state press and government officials openly talked about the problem of illegal detention in "black jails." The government claimed that it was cracking down and persecuting people who ran "black jails," and it made a few scapegoats. But now government officials simply deny the existence of "black jails." Chinese diplomats did just that when asked during the UN Human Rights Council's Universal Periodic Review in October and during the UN Committee on Rights of the Child's review of China's treaty obligations in September. Have "black jails" disappeared? Not really. They continue to operate even in the nation's capital. We have seen many reports of their existence.

Mr. LIU. Any other questions from the audience? Oh, Susan, actually, back there in the red. Go ahead.

PARTICIPANT. I have something short, because I missed Professor Fewsmith in the beginning. It took me a long time to struggle down here.

Mr. FEWSMITH. I can repeat.

PARTICIPANT. Well, I'll get you afterward. But did somebody talk about the law of open government information, the regulation, I mean? Because underlying all of this is an absence of reliable information. I remember when I was watching that regulation in the beginning, the cases would be rarely accepted, or if they were accepted they would be thrown out for a small reason. So if somebody were watching that, it really is the—[inaudible], I think, in thinking that's the key to getting corruption under control. Anybody have thoughts on that?

Mr. FEWSMITH. I'll take a crack at that. I haven't done a lot of work on that, but I remember after hearing about them I went down to Guangdong, which is one of the places where it seems to have been implemented, and I had a long interview with somebody who had been involved in it. It was very clear that there was not much there. It just was not being implemented in a very concrete way, according to him.

PARTICIPANT. We did have a draft that went to various different provinces. One of them was a lady in central China who is famous for doing information laws. We went to these places and tried to do a clinical program in a couple of local law schools and help students with those kinds of suits. But it turned out to be that, nobody wanted—professors didn't want to prosecute that kind of suit. They felt they would be retaliated against. I think the fear is of retaliation. So maybe there is something to be done to address that.

Mr. FEWSMITH. Yes.

Mr. LIU. Okay. I think we have time for one more question. This gentleman on the left here.

PARTICIPANT. You mentioned some of the proceeds of corrupt payments flowing offshore into U.S. real estate markets. I was wondering if any of the panelists might be able to discuss further some of the corporate and financial plumbing that is involved in facilitating and concealing the payments.

Mr. WEDEMAN. That's a tough one. I have had descriptions of how the money flows. It's complicated. Who knows if the stories are true or not. The money flows in the same way that narcotics money flows. I was told that somebody could arrange to take a tractor trailer full of renminbi across the border into Hong Kong. That was the point where I felt that the conversation was going in a direction that I really didn't want to know much more.

Money moves around the Cayman Islands, the Jersey Islands, the Bahamas, lots of shell companies. Good lawyers with not-so-great ethics will get you money moved around the world. But yes, I assume there are multiple subterranean channels.

Mr. CHOW. But the U.S. Government, the U.S. Attorney's Office, as well as the Department of Justice is very good at asset recovery if they have some information, but they need to have more information that they are getting from the Chinese Government in order to go after these assets.

Mr. LIU. Well, I think we have gone over by a few minutes. We started a little late. So I wanted to end the proceeding here and thank the witnesses, each of you, for your excellent, insightful presentations and responses to the questions, and thank the audience for coming today.

This roundtable is adjourned.

[Whereupon, at 4:41 p.m., the roundtable was adjourned.]

APPENDIX

PREPARED STATEMENTS

PREPARED STATEMENT OF ANDREW WEDEMAN

XI JINPING'S ANTI-CORRUPTION CAMPAIGN AND THE THIRD PLENUM[1]

NOVEMBER 21, 2013

A year ago, Xi Jinping assumed the office of General Secretary of the Communist Party of China (CCP) in the wake of the most serious corruption scandal since 2006 when Shanghai Municipal Party Secretary Chen Liangyu was caught diverting upwards of Y40 billion (US$4.8 billion) from the municipal pension fund to speculative real estate and financial investments. In February 2012, Wang Lijun, who had headed the Chongqing Public Security Bureau until being abruptly "re-assigned" four days earlier to head the city's educational and environmental offices, fled to the US Consulate in Chengdu allegedly in hopes of obtaining political asylum in the United States. Wang's failed "defection" brought to light allegations that Politburo member and Chongqing Municipal Party Secretary Bo Xilai's wife Gu Kailai had murdered an English businessman in an out of the way Chongqing hotel. In the weeks that followed, the Chinese rumor mill buzzed about possible coup plots involving Bo and the head of the party's legal and security committee Zhou Yongkang. Wang, Gu, and Bo was subsequently convicted of bribery, embezzlement, and abuse of power, with Wang also being convicted of treason. Coming hard on the heels of a scandal involving the former Minister of Railways Liu Zhijun, the Bo case put Xi under tremendous pressure to launch a major anti-corruption campaign as soon as he entered office. In his first speech as CCP General Secretary, Xi declared:

> There are many pressing problems within the Party that needs to be resolved urgently, especially the graft and corruption cases that occurred to some of the Party members and cadres, being out of touch from the general public, bureaucracy and undue emphasis on formalities—they must be resolved with great efforts. The whole Party must be vigilant against them. To forge iron, one must be strong. Our responsibility is to work with all comrades in the party, to make sure the party supervises its own conduct and enforces strict discipline . . . (CNN, 11/15/2012).

In a subsequent address to the Politburo, Xi doubled down, saying:

> A mass of facts tells us that if corruption becomes increasingly serious, it will inevitably doom the party and the state. We must be vigilant. In recent years, there have been cases of grave violations of disciplinary rules and laws within the party that have been extremely malign in nature and utterly destructive politically, shocking people to the core. (NYT, 11/19/2012).

Strong words, however, only have meaning if they are translated into concrete actions. As the party approaches its Third Plenum a key question is how vigorously has Xi attacked high level corruption over the past year?

Measuring the intensity of an anti-corruption campaign is difficult. Absent any way of measuring the actual rate of corruption it is impossible to know if inroads are being made into the number of officials who are corrupt. It is possible, however, to crudely track changes in the intensity of enforcement by looking at changes in the reported number of officials detained. Figures released in October 2013 on the number of corruption cases "filed" by the Procuratorate suggest that the total number of cases was up about 3.8% in the first eight months of 2013 compared to the same period in 2012. Other figures released by the Procuratorate for all of 2012, however, reported a 5.4% increase in cases filed that year and a 6.4% increase in the number of individuals charged. If the two sets of data are comparable, which they may not be, the more recent data would suggest that Xi's anti-corruption campaign has not produced much of an increase in the number of officials charged with corruption. Moreover, past experience suggests that using partial year figures to extrapolate totals for the year tends yield overestimates. It thus seems likely that Xi's new campaign will not produce a significant increase in the number of corruption cases filed but will instead yield numbers approximately equal to those we have seen over the past decade (see Figure 1).

---

[1] Originally posted by the China Policy Institute - University of Nottingham, available on line at http://blogs.nottingham.ac.uk/chinapolicyinstitute/2013/11/15/xi-jinpings-anti-corruption-campaign-and-the-third-plenum/.

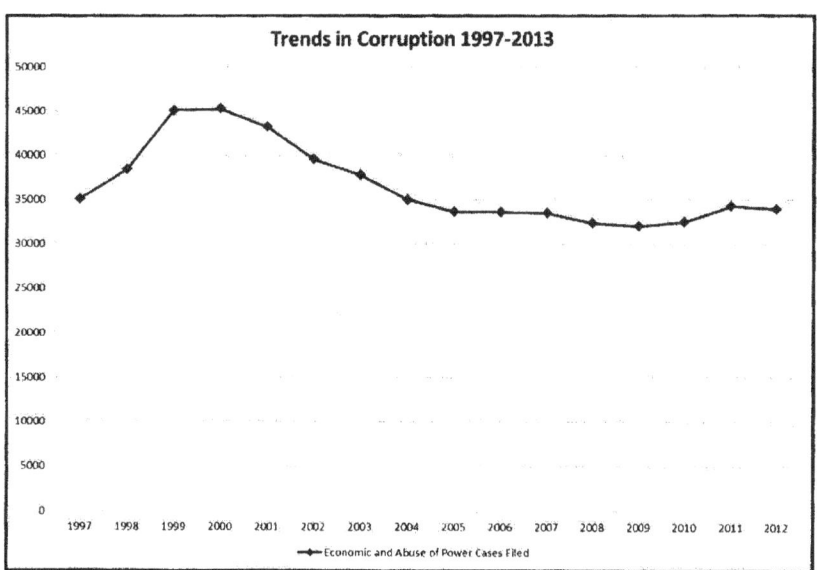

Numbers, however, tell only part of the story. To more fully assess Xi's anti-corruption campaign, one must look at who has been targeted. According to press reports, thus far Xi's campaign has claimed eight "tigers"—high level, high profile officials (see Table 1). Eight senior officials is about the number of senior officials indicted on corruption charges in recent years (five were indicted in 2012, seven in 2011, six in 2010, and eight in 2009). Xi's campaign has, however, also snared a number of senior executives of major state-owned companies, including over half a dozen executives of the China National Petroleum Corp (CNPC) and its subsidiaries Sinopec and PetroChina, as well as a number of mid-level officials and business persons linked to Li Chuncheng, a former Deputy Secretary of the Sichuan Provincial Party Committee. Arrests of executives, in fact, are one of the few aspects of the current campaign that set it apart from previous drives.

Table 1	
Big Tigers	
Li Chuncheng	Deputy Party Secretary, Sichuan
Liu Tienan	Vice Minister State Development and Reform Commission
Wu Yongwen	Deputy Director Hubei People's Congress Standing Committee
General Gu Junshan	Deputy Commander PLA General Logistics Department
Huang Sheng	Vice Governor Shandong
Ni Fake	Vice Governor Anhui
Tian Xueren	Vice Governor Jilin
General Xi Caihou	Vice Chairman PLA Central Military Commission

Many of those detained have direct or indirect ties to former Politburo Standing Committee member Zhou Yongkang (see Figure 2). A native of Wuxi in Jiangsu, Zhou was trained as a petroleum engineer in the mid-1960s and worked in the Liaohe oilfields in Liaoning until he was appointed Vice Minister of the Ministry of Petroleum Industry in 1983. Five years later, he moved to CNPC, servicing as deputy party secretary and then party secretary before becoming its General Manager in 1996. A year later, he was elected a full member of the 15th CCP Central Committee. In 1998, he was appointed Minister for Land and Resources but then moved to Sichuan to become secretary of the provincial party committee in 1999. Four years later, he returned to Beijing when he was appointed Minister for Public Security and became a member of the Politburo at the 16th Party Congress. In 2007, he left the Ministry of Public Security to become the Secretary and then Director of the Central Committee's powerful Politics and Law Commission, a position that put Zhou in charge of China's internal security and police apparatus, and was elected a member of the Politburo Standing Committee, positions he held until the 18th Party Congress in 2012, at which point he retired. In the course of his career Zhou apparently built up a sprawling network of protégés in the oil, resources, and security apparatus. In the spring of 2012, he was rumored to be connected to Bo Xilai and his campaign to gain a seat on the Politburo Standing Committee. Today, many see Zhou as a threat to General Secretary Xi Jinping's efforts to consolidate power within the leadership. It is widely speculated, therefore, that Xi's anti-corruption campaign is actually a cover for a major drive against Zhou and his allies. Some observers have, in fact, linked the announcement of a new National Security Council as Xi's attempt to bypass Zhou's allies in the party's Law and Politics apparatus.

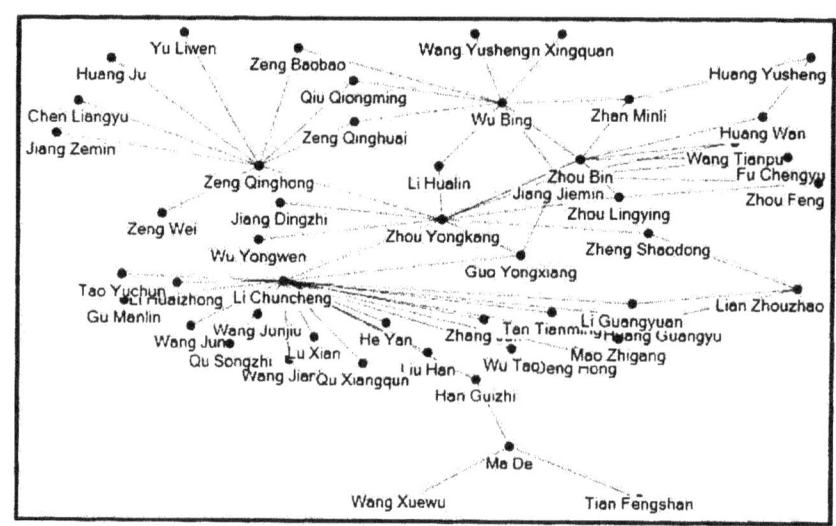

Targeting Zhou and his allies is, however, a potentially dicey proposition because Zhou has ties to Zeng Qinghong, a former member of the Politburo Standing Committee, who is said to have played a major role in Zhou's accent to the inner leadership. Zeng, who worked in the petroleum sector before moving to the Shanghai municipal party committee in 1984, is considered be to one of Jiang Zemin's "Shanghai Gang," a group that also includes former Politburo Standing Committee member Huang Ju and former Shanghai party secretary Chen Liangyu, the latter now serving an eighteen years sentence after being convicted of corruption in 2008. Should Xi opt to take down Zhou, there could be a considerable risk that he would foment a major political backlash lead by some of the party's most powerful elders.

If part of the current anti-corruption campaign is being driven by Xi's need to consolidate his power within the leadership and respond to public pressures for a new drive against corruption unleashed by the Bo case, the dynamics of the campaign have been driven in part by forces that Xi does not control. Over the past several years, social media has played an increasingly important role in exposing corrupt officials. During the early days of the current campaign, reports on the internet fingering officials for owning multiple luxury apartments, sporting luxury watches, and engaging in immoral activity led to a series of quick resignations, sackings, and arrests. Most of those exposed on the internet were mid or low-level officials. Nevertheless, social media had made it impossible for these sorts of officials to quickly sweep allegations against them under the rug and quash attempts to expose their wrongdoing. The threat of uncontrolled outings clearly spooked the regime, which responded with draconian regulations that would criminalize those who spread "rumors" on the internet. Thus far, it appears that the new rules have had a chilling effect and there has been a notable dropping off in social media reports of corruption.

At the Third Plenum in November 2013, corruption received surprisingly little attention. Xi did not take the opportunity to report dramatic progress or to unveil bold new measures designed to curb corruption. Instead, he opted to stress economic reform and announced reforms of the judicial system designed to increase its independence from the political establishment. The lack of attention to corruption during the plenum likely signals Xi's anti-corruption campaign has run its course and that it will be allowed to quietly die down. Based on the available evidence, the campaign does not seem to have made noticeable inroads into China's corruption problem. A lack of dramatic progress is, ultimately, hardly surprising. A war on corruption is by definition a protracted fight in which the regime "wins" by preventing corruption from worsening. The officials caught in the current campaign did not become corrupt under Xi. On the contrary, most had been on the take for years or even decades. As such, Xi is now fighting to clean up a mess created under his predecessors, neither of whom made great strides toward eradicating corruption.

––––––––––

PREPARED STATEMENT OF DANIEL C.K. CHOW

CHINA'S CRACKDOWN ON COMMERCIAL BRIBERY, CORRUPTION IN STATE-OWNED EN-TERPRISES, AND THE IMPACT ON U.S.-BASED MULTINATIONAL COMPANIES DOING BUSINESS IN CHINA

NOVEMBER 21, 2013

The recent high profile crackdown on commercial bribery by China may result in increased legal risks to U.S.-based multinational companies (MNCs) doing business in China. Commercial bribery, further defined below, often involves a state-owned enterprise (SOE) as one of the actors in the bribery transaction. China's SOEs are known for their culture of corruption in which SOEs both give and receive bribes as a matter of course in doing business on a daily basis. As part of the crackdown on commercial bribery, China has issued an important legal interpretation that emphasizes enforcement against the payor of a bribe. This could indicate a shift in emphasis because China has been primarily concerned so far with focusing on the recipient of the bribe. A focus on the payor of the bribe could expose MNCs to liability because MNCs are often the payor of bribes to SOEs and government officials. Although this crackdown is not publicly aimed at U.S. and other foreign multinational companies, this crackdown creates a significant increased risk for U.S.-based multinational companies doing business in China. The highest risk is not in China's prosecution of its anti-bribery laws, but in prosecution by the U.S. Department of Justice and the Securities and Exchange Commission for violations of the Foreign Corruption Practices Act (FCPA),[1] a federal law that prohibits the giving of bribes by U.S. companies to foreign officials for the purpose of obtaining or retaining business. As further explained below, the crackdown by Chinese authorities will expose practices, now hidden, which might be considered by the United States to violate the FCPA and result in an FCPA investigation. The United States regularly monitors the Chinese media and any serious national crackdown will draw the attention of U.S. authorities.

I. CRACKDOWN ON COMMERCIAL BRIBERY

President Xi Jinping became China's head of state on March 14, 2013, a once in a decade transition of power. On November 18, 2002, he warned that "corruption could kill the party and ruin the country," a sentiment reiterated repeatedly at local levels. President Xi warned that he would target "tigers and lilies"—high level as well as low level officials. As part of this anti-corruption campaign, China seems now to be intensifying its crackdown on commercial bribery. On November 20, 2008, the Supreme People Court's and the Supreme People's Procuratorate jointly issued an interpretation focusing on commercial bribery[2] and, more recently, on December

––––––––––

[1] See 15 U.S.C. §§ 78m et seq. (2006).

[2] Opinions of the Supreme People's Court and the Supreme People's Procuratorate on Certain Issues concerning the Application of Law in Handling Criminal Cases of Commercial Bribery (effective on November 20, 2008).

26, 2012, both institutions also issued an opinion, effective as of January 1, 2013, focusing criminal prosecution of the payor of the bribe.[3] China also recently announced a sweeping investigation of the pharmaceutical sector focusing on MNCs giving bribes to doctors and administrations of state owned hospitals for the purpose of influencing the doctors and officials to buy their pharmaceuticals. Local officials in Guangdong Province, a regional economic powerhouse, publicly announced their intention to crack down on commercial bribery, among other economic crimes.

In this context, commercial bribery refers to a transaction in which the payor, usually a business entity, gives the recipient a bribe in order to obtain business or some other illegitimate business benefit. In many cases, both of the actors, the payor and the recipient, are business entities. These are business-to-business corruption cases or commercial bribery, an area of recent focus by China, which differs from government corruption. An example of commercial bribery is when an employee of one company that sells commodities gives a kickback to an employee of a company that purchases commodities. Another example is when the payor of the bribe gives cash to a vice director of the Ministry of Railways in order to obtain business, such as a contract to build a high speed train. This is also the gift of a bribe in order to obtain business so is considered to be commercial bribery. The key element in commercial bribery is the use of the use of a bribe to obtain business or another illegitimate benefit related to business. Contrast this type of transaction with a transaction in which both actors are government entities such as a state oil company and a state bank. The bank lends money to the state oil company to buy a foreign oil field but the loan is for a greater amount than the market value of the oil field. An official from the state-owned oil company keeps the extra amount of the loan and deposits the amount in his private offshore account. This would be an example of government graft or corruption. While China has focused on government graft, the Chinese government appears to now be focusing in addition on commercial bribery.

II. COMMERCIAL BRIBERY AND STATE-OWNED ENTERPRISES

Since commercial bribery often involves a company-to-company transaction, an MNC and an SOE are often involved in the transaction. An MNC is involved on one end as the payor of the bribe and an SOE on the other end as the recipient of the bribe. Several factors indicate that with China's increased attention on commercial bribery, U.S.-based MNCs will be exposed to additional legal risk. As noted earlier, the greatest risk is not with the prosecution by Chinese authorities of its anti-bribery laws, but with exposure under the Foreign Corrupt Practices Act. There is increased exposure for the following reasons.

A. State-Owned Enterprises and the Business Culture of Corruption

State-owned enterprises are "business entities established by central and local governments and whose supervisory officials are from the government."[4] Most people in China believe that SOEs commonly give and receive bribes when they do business. Most people in China accept petty corruption by SOEs and other government officials as a way of doing business. Many MNCs must constantly do business with SOEs because SOEs dominate in all core industries in China: petroleum and gas, financial services, including banking and insurance; automotive; electric, gas and water; real estate development, metals, mining, and telecommunications. When SOEs engage in procurement (i.e. buying commodities) or selling commodities, they often use bribes, gifts, and favors as part of the transaction. When MNCs deal with SOEs, MNCs often face demands for payments, gifts, and favors made by low level or mid-level employees at SOEs. For example, in a commercial bribery transaction, a sales agent from an MNC might feel pressure to give a kickback or bribe to the purchasing agent of an SOE to induce the purchasing agent to place an order to buy products from the sales agent and the MNC. From the perspective of the purchasing agent of the SOE, it makes little difference whether the agent places an order with any particular supplier since the purchasing agent, a low level employee, receives a fixed salary. The kickback or bribe serves as an inducement to the purchasing agent to place the order with the MNC because it gives the purchasing agent extra cash.

---

[3] The Interpretation of the Supreme People's Court and the Supreme People's Procuratorate of Several Issues Concerning the Specific Application of the Law in the Handling of Criminal Bribery Cases (effective as of January 1, 2013).

[4] State Owned Enterprises in China: Reviewing the Evidence, OECD Working Group on Privatisation and Corporate Governance of State Owned Assets 3 (Jan. 26, 2009)

Under the FCPA, U.S. companies are prohibited from giving bribes to "foreign officials"[5] for the purpose of obtain or retaining business. The U.S. Department of Justice considers all employees of SOEs from the highest ranking to the lowest to be "foreign officials." This could well mean that a kickback or bribe given by an MNC to a SOE will be viewed as a bribe to a foreign official and trigger liability under the FCPA. With the increased emphasis on commercial bribery and on payors of bribes, Chinese authorities might begin an investigation against the MNC for paying bribes. This could draw the attention of the U.S. Department of Justice, which could then begin an investigation under the FCPA.

B. "Anything of Value"

The FCPA prohibits the giving of not just money but "anything of value"[6] in order to obtain or retain business. Under China's own anti-bribery laws, a payor must give "money or property" to be guilty of a bribe.[7] In China's current and traditional business culture, the giving of favors is viewed as a common form of doing business; many employees in SOEs and in MNCs may not view giving a non-monetary gift or a favor for a family member—such as giving an internship to the daughter of a government official—as doing anything illegal or wrong, but the same type of action might be viewed by the U.S. Department of Justice as giving something of value in violation of the FCPA.

C. Dealing with Third Parties

Many MNCs find that they must do business with third parties or hire third party independent contractors on a regular basis in China. In many instances, a U.S.-based MNC sets up a joint venture in China with an SOE as the joint venture partner. In this context, the joint venture is a China business entity formed under Chinese law and is jointly owned by the MNC and the local partner, often an SOE. The MNC contributes capital and technology and the local partner contributes its knowledge of the local market and its business and official connections. In some industries, joint ventures are required by law; an MNC is not permitted to set up a wholly foreign owned subsidiary but must partner with a local Chinese company. If the local partner is an SOE, the SOE might be used to giving bribes as part of how it did business in the past and once it becomes a partner in the joint venture, the SOE local partner might continue to give bribes to secure business from other SOEs or from government entities. This is exactly what happened to RAE Systems, a Delaware corporation, which formed several joint ventures with local SOEs. RAE had a majority interest in the joint ventures while the SOEs had a minority interest. The joint venture made chemical and radiation detectors and sold them to various government bureaus and departments. Before they entered into the joint ventures with RAE, the Chinese SOEs were paying bribes (kickbacks) to government bureaus to obtain sales. After they entered into the joint ventures, the Chinese employees from the SOEs continued to give kickbacks not only in money but in the form of jade, fur coats, kitchen appliances, and business suits. The actions of the joint ventures (as the agents of RAE) are attributable to RAE, the parent company under the FCPA. The U.S. Department of Justice intended to charge RAE with violations of the FCPA but the parties settled the case.

MNCs also have a common practice of hiring third parties as consultants for their China business entities. These third parties can be business consultants, public relations firms, private investigation companies, or lawyers. These third party consultants have been known to make payments (bribes) to government officials on behalf of the MNC and report the bribe to the MNC as a miscellaneous expense. The FCPA has a provision that giving money or anything of value to a third party knowing that the money will be given to a foreign official can constitute an FCPA violation.[8]

III. CONSEQUENCES ON THE CRACKDOWN ON COMMERCIAL BRIBERY

China's recent crackdown on commercial bribery could expose MNCs to increased legal exposure, but the highest exposure does not lie in China's enforcement of its laws against MNCs but in the U.S. Department of Justice's enforcement of the FCPA against MNCs. The Chinese government sees a political and strategic value in cracking down on commercial bribery. In any bribery case, there are two choke points: it is possible to pursue the payor/giver of the bribe and also the recipient/

---

[5] See 15 U.S.C. §§ 78dd-1(a)(1), 78dd-2(a)(1), 78dd-3(a)(1).

[6] See 15 U.S.C. §§ 78dd-1(a), 78dd-2(a), 78dd-3(a).

[7] See, e.g., Article 389 PRC Criminal Law (1997) ("Whoever, for the purpose of securing illegitimate benefits, gives money or property to a state functionary shall be guilty of offering bribes.").

[8] See 15 U.S.C. §§78dd-1(3), 78dd-2(a)(3), 78dd-3(a)(3).

taker of the bribe. So far China's emphasis has been on the recipient/taker of the bribe. In many cases, the recipient of the bribe can be a government official and a member of the Communist Party. In pursuing the recipient of the bribe, the Communist Party risks embarrassment as its own members are exposed as corrupt. A related risk to the CPC is any Party member that is accused of receiving a bribe might implicate other Party members higher in the Party order. From the Party's perspective, pursuing a commercial bribery case against an MNC carries fewer political risks but will also serve a political and symbolic purpose in demonstrating to the public that the Party is serious about cracking down on corruption. However, the CPC does not wish to inflict serious penalties on MNCs. Although the CPC might pursue individual executives within an MNC and even impose prison sentences on such executives, the CPC is unlikely to shut down the MNCs. Many MNCs have invested substantial capital and technology in their foreign-invested enterprises in China. The CPC realizes that shutting down or inflicting serious losses on MNCs and disrupting their businesses will ultimately harm China's economy and China's own long term interests. On the other hand, the penalties under the FCPA can be significant and can include terms of imprisonment for U.S.-based directors or officers of the company. The U.S. Department of Justice can also impose heavy monetary penalties. In recent cases, the U.S. Department of Justice settled an FCPA investigation with Total SA, a French company, for $398 million and with JGC Corp. for $218.8 million. In addition, any U.S. company that is the subject of an investigation by the U.S. Department of Justice could suffer immediate adverse publicity.

IV. CONCLUSION

The increased emphasis on enforcement against commercial bribery, which often involves an SOE as the recipient of the bribe, and a shift in emphasis on enforcement against the payor of the bribe (as opposed to the recipient) might pose significantly higher risks to MNCs doing business in China. The highest risk is not prosecution under China's anti-bribery laws for commercial bribery but prosecutions under the FCPA, which has much stiffer monetary penalties and also the possibility of imprisonment for U.S. executives involved directly or indirectly in the giving of the bribe.

○